I0794260

Rescue That Cat!

by Linda Smith
illustrated by Kersti Frigell

Core Decodable 83

McGraw Hill Education

Bothell, WA • Chicago, IL • Columbus, OH • New York, NY

MHEonline.com

Copyright © 2015 McGraw-Hill Education

All rights reserved. No part of this publication may be reproduced or distributed in any form or by any means, or stored in a database or retrieval system, without the prior written consent of McGraw-Hill Education, including, but not limited to, network storage or transmission, or broadcast for distance learning.

Send all inquiries to:
McGraw-Hill Education
8787 Orion Place
Columbus, OH 43240

ISBN: 978-0-02-144878-4
MHID: 0-02-144878-7

Printed in Canada.

9 10 11 12 KOD 24

A cat mews in a tree.
Will you rescue that cat?

The cat continues to mew.

I will rescue the cat.

You will rescue the cat?

No, I will rescue the cat.

Few like the cat as much as I do.

Let's not argue. We all value the cat.
You can rescue the cat.

Yes, let's not argue. Few value the cat like you.

You can rescue the cat.

Do not argue. We all value the cat.
She will rescue the cat. The cat mews.